ADVANCED LAW OF ATTRACTION

AND ATTRACTING WHAT YOU WANT FAST.

This book is dedicated to those people who have shared their Law of Attraction success stories and insights with me. Their success demonstrates the great truth that the Law of Attraction works if you work it.

THE LAW OF ATTRACTION WORKS...IF YOU WORK IT!

The fastest way to manifest your desires is by implementing a Law of Attraction action plan. Since everything in the Universe is energy, the necessary ingredient for manifestation is the consistent mental and emotional energy that you emit in the form of thoughts, feelings, words and actions. It's very important to remember that the phrase "Law of Attraction" contains the word ACTION. Too many people on this spiritual path get caught up reading lots of books about the Law of Attraction, attending numerous seminars and hearing lectures about the Universal Law, but they fail to use the powerful tools that will translate their desires from the invisible world of cause to the visible world of manifestation. There are many books and audio programs on the market that explain what the Law of Attraction is and what it does, but few that actually teach people how to use this creative power on a daily basis. As a result, this book will provide you with advanced manifestation techniques, strategies, insights, and success stories that will help you quickly manifest your desires with the Law of Attraction.

The manifestation of your desires will take place slowly or quickly depending upon your commitment to the manifestation process and your ability to align to this power by creating an intention that feels believable to you, implementing a Law of Attraction action plan, and then moving into alignment with this dynamic power until your desire has appeared. The commitment to speed up your manifestation requires 100% dedication, but the wonderful promise is that the Law of Attraction can and will deliver your desire as long as you provide the consistent mental and emotional energy that is required for the manifestation process. What you desire must show up in your life because the Universal Law cannot ignore your intention for a greater, more abundant expression of life, which includes money, opportunities, success, romance, and all the good things you desire. The Universal Law, which is a part of you, is expansive and evolutionary by its very nature, and its purpose is to guide and direct your human evolution in a way that provides you the opportunity to grow mentally, emotionally, spiritually, and in ways that support a greater expression of life. Your desire for more money, love, and personal fulfillment is an inherent, evolutionary impulse to become more of the person you are meant to be as you experience greater levels of spiritual awareness.

WHY YOU SHOULD READ THIS BOOK

Many Law of Attraction students have expressed concerns about being overwhelmed with all the manifestation books and study materials on the market. A friend recently told me: "I went to a book store and saw so many Law of Attraction books that I couldn't decide which to buy." Another friend said, "I know what the Law of Attraction is and what it does, but I am having trouble understanding what I need to do each day to make it work for me." I responded by telling my friend that she is not alone with her concerns. There is a lot of information on the market explaining what the Law of Attraction does, yet much of it fails to explain what must be done on a daily basis to make it work effectively. As a result of these concerns, I have written this book to guide readers through a series of real-life, daily scenarios that demonstrate what should be done each day in order to use the Law of Attraction effectively. The people interviewed for this book are among hundreds of people whom I have met during the course of my spiritual journey. I have met these wonderful people at seminars, workshops, lectures, churches, spiritual centers and through online forums on spirituality and personal growth. These enlightened individuals are among my growing community of spiritual friends who have shared their insights and experiences with me, and who comprise a growing support group of like-minded people who understand the importance of self-empowerment and spiritual evolution.

WHAT THIS BOOK CONTAINS:

PART 1 contains a detailed list of advanced Law of Attraction techniques required to manifest your desires quickly. PART 2 contains detailed interviews, insights and strategies of individuals who have manifested money, success and opportunities with the Law of Attraction. PART 3 contains detailed interviews, insights and strategies of individuals who have manifested romance and friends with the Law of Attraction. PART 4 includes the common denominators of each successful manifestation and other helpful information that can be used to accelerate the manifestation process. PART 5 includes a detailed question and answer section that covers some of the most important questions about the manifestation process. PART 6 includes information that will assist in creating your Law of Attraction action plan, including tips and suggestions to follow throughout the day as you implement a practical, daily schedule that is enjoyable and effective.

TABLE OF CONTENTS:

PART 1: Advanced Law of Attraction Techniques

PART 2: Manifesting Desires - Interviews with people who have manifested money, success and opportunities with the Law of Attraction

PART 3: Manifesting Love and Friends - Interviews with people who have manifested love and friends with the Law of Attraction

PART 4: Common Denominators of Successful Manifestations

PART 5: Question and Answer Section

PART 6: Creating and Implementing Your Daily Law of Attraction Action Plan

PART 1: The Advanced Law of Attraction Techniques

There are a number of metaphysical tools and daily practices that will speed up the manifestation process if used consistently. The tools covered in this section include the Intention Statement, Vision Board, Emotional Visualization, Allowing Statement, and the Belief Statement. This section will provide insights that will explain how to use these advanced Law of Attraction techniques in order to accelerate the manifestation process whether you want to manifest love, more money, or success on a continual basis.

ADVANCED LAW OF ATTRACTION TECHNIQUE #1: INTENTION STATEMENT

One of the most powerful Law of Attraction tools you can use to speed up the manifestation process is an Intention Statement. An Intention Statement, when used daily and persistently, is so powerful that it can literally cut your manifestation time in half. Although numerous authors have written about the creative power of spoken affirmations, many have failed to explain that a properly used Intention Statement helps focus our thoughts, feelings, and expectations on the things we want to manifest. And we all know that energy flows where attention goes.

I first learned how to use an Intention Statement when I was in my mid-twenties. At that time I was a new student of metaphysics and very eager to learn as much as possible about the art of manifestation. As a result, I attended numerous Law of Attraction workshops at spiritual book stores throughout Southern California. At one of these workshops I met an insightful teacher who introduced me to the creative power of the Intention Statement. Heather was a prosperous woman who had been studying metaphysics since she was in her early twenties. No matter how busy she was throughout the day, she always made time to use an Intention Statement and the other tools of manifestation. One of the most important facts she taught me about the Law of Attraction was that in order to master manifestation I must be clear about my *intention* and then give it my committed, daily *attention* until the manifestation has taken place. We cannot expect to manifest our desires if our commitment is wishy-washy. The only way to manifest desires is by focusing upon them consistently until we have established the belief and expectation to translate them from the realm of thought to the realm of manifestation. We do this by using a Law of Attraction Action Plan that includes the use of an Intention Statement.

HOW TO CREATE A POWERFUL INTENTION STATEMENT:

The most powerful Intention Statements are short and to the point. Your statement should be a concise, accurate reflection of exactly what you want to manifest, and it should be short enough to easily remember and repeat throughout the day while visualizing, meditating or whenever the thought arises. Intention Statements that are short and to-the-point are much easier to remember and repeat than long statements that require a lot of time and mental effort to repeat. You will use your Intention Statement several times per day, so be sure that the words you choose feel good to you. If your Intention Statement makes you feel good, excited and expectant then you are on the right track.

Some of my favorite Intention Statements are as follows:

- My intention is to have an abundance of money so that I can save at least $2,000.00 per month.

- My intention is to attract a kind and loving mate so that I can enjoy romance and companionship throughout my life.

- My intention is to manifest a wonderful job that is fulfilling, utilizes my talents, and pays me well.

- My intention is to have more than enough money to take wonderful, exciting trips around the world every year.

Although you can use the Intention Statements that are provided, you should create your own statement because the words that reflect your feelings are the most powerful words you can use. If your intention does not "feel right" for you or if you cannot mentally and emotionally accept certain words and possibilities at this time, then you should change your statement to reflect something that feels better for you right now. For example, if the intention to be a millionaire within five years does not feel possible right now, then you might want to change your statement to reflect a reality that you can currently accept. You may want to use an Intention Statement such as: MY INTENTION IS TO ALWAYS HAVE LOTS OF MONEY SO THAT I CAN SAVE AT LEAST $2,000.00 PER MONTH, DRIVE THE CAR OF MY DREAMS, AND

EXPERIENCE A LIFE OF COMFORT AND EASE. As you persist in using the tools of manifestation and as your expectation increases, you can change your Intention Statement to reflect your evolving beliefs, feelings and expectations. Your Intention Statement can change as you manifest one desire and then set your aim on another intention. For example, a friend named Jessica spent much of her free time alone, so she created an Intention Statement for the purpose of attracting quality friends. Her Intention Statement was, "MY INTENTION IS TO ATTRACT RELIABLE, QUALITY FRIENDS TO FILL MY EVENINGS AND WEEKENDS WITH FUN TIMES AND WONDERFUL MEMORIES." As she took the time to focus on her Intention Statement each day, she noticed that she was receiving more invites to socialize with coworkers, classmates, and people she greeted at the local coffee shop each morning. Eventually, she met a lady who shared a similar interest in books. Through that lady, Jessica was introduced to a group of ladies in a local book club that met twice a month. Soon Jessica's evening and weekend schedules were filled with reliable, quality friends and wonderful memories. About a year later, Jessica felt that she was ready to expand her social circle by including romance in her busy social life, so she replaced her Intention Statement with a new one, "MY INTENTION IS TO ATTRACT THE PERFECT MAN WHO IS ROMANTIC, CARING AND FUN TO BE WITH." Six months later, she met a man who was ready for a committed relationship. As the new relationship blossomed, Jessica and her boyfriend Sam got engaged exactly two years after their first date. They eventually got married in Laguna Beach, California.

HOW TO USE YOUR INTENTION STATEMENT:

Once you have created an Intention Statement that makes you feel good, you should repeat it several times per day with feeling. The shorter the statement, the easier it will be to repeat as you go about your busy schedule each day. You should repeat your Intention Statement at least three times per day, but more often if time permits. For the first few days you might want to repeat your statement in the morning, during the middle of the day, and again before bedtime. As you get into the habit of using your Intention Statement and as your expectation increases, you should repeat it more often throughout the day. A person who is committed to mastering manifestation will find that she repeats her Intention Statement up to a dozen times per day. A friend in San Francisco repeats his Intention Statement several times per day as he commutes to work, lifts weights at the gym, and prepares his dinner in the evening. He has manifested several intentions with the Law of Attraction, including the career of his dreams, financial prosperity, and romance. A female friend who uses her Intention Statement to maintain focus and expectancy, has manifested love, money, business success and a busy social life through her dedication to the Law of Attraction. In an e-mail message, she shared some valuable information about her daily ritual: "I repeated my Intention Statement several times a day even when I didn't feel like it. Now I know that the Universe responds to persistence because I got everything I wanted."

Intention Statements are not magic spells. They serve the purpose of focusing your words, thoughts and feelings on what you want to manifest. Since the Universal Law will deliver what you think about consistently, you must give attention to the things you desire on a regular basis. The reason that many people fail at manifesting intentions is that too little time is spent thinking about and focusing on their intentions. As a result, part of your Law of Attraction action plan should be to use your Intention Statement several times per day. You might want to write your statement on a small card so that you will be reminded to focus on your desires throughout the day. A lady whom I interviewed wrote her Intention Statement on a small card and then had it laminated. She placed the card on her desk as a reminder to focus on her Intention Statement daily.

ADVANCED LAW OF ATTRACTION TECHNIQUE #2: HOW TO USE A VISION BOARD

For decades, spiritual writers and mystics have written about the creative power of a Vision Board, also called a Treasure Map or a Goal Map. The purpose of a Vision Board is to display images of the things you want to achieve, have or experience in life. When used properly, it is a very powerful manifestation tool because it helps you clarify, concentrate and maintain focus on your intentions. Vision Boards are so popular that many business professionals, entertainers, celebrities, entrepreneurs and students have used them for success in many different areas of life. In fact, many popular authors such as Bob Proctor and John Assaraf have written about the creative power of a Vision Board.

In order to make a Vision Board you will need some cardstock that measures 8 ½ x 11 inches or larger depending upon the size you feel comfortable using. You don't have to spend a lot of money to create a Vision Board because cardstock is relatively inexpensive at most stationery stores. In addition, you will need a number of images that reflect the things you want to experience in life. You can cut out images from magazines, print them off the Internet, or you can use photographs. A friend from New York City who is a Broadway actor used images taken from Playbills and theatrical magazines to represent the success he desired as a stage actor. Another friend, who owns the home of his dreams, used images taken from real estate magazines to help him focus on the reality of owning his dream home. In addition, he added statements to his Vision Board such as "MY INTENTION IS TO MANIFEST THE HOME OF MY DREAMS" and "IT FEELS GOOD TO LIVE IN MY DREAM HOUSE." Both friends quickly manifested their desires because they regularly spent time focusing on their Vision Boards while feeling the reality of their fulfilled desire.

When choosing images for your Vision Board it is very important to use images that make you feel good. For example, if you find a picture of a house that does not appeal to you, you should continue searching until you find a picture of another house that feels more like "home." The same rules apply to using your Vision Board to attract the perfect mate. If certain images do not feel right, then use different images that encourage you to feel positive and expectant. As you search for images to post on your board, you will find that certain ones make you feel better than others. You must always follow your hunches when creating a Vision Board because hunches originate within your higher self, which speaks the language of feelings. For example, a friend who wanted to manifest lots of money did not feel positive and expectant when looking at the images of money on her board. As a result, I suggested that she add more images of the things she wanted to buy, experience, and do with the money. After following my advice, she reported feeling much better about her Vision Board. Within a few months, she manifested her desire because she took time each day to focus on feeling the reality of her desires. These rules also apply to the words and phrases that you will post on your Vision Board. Once you have sorted through magazines to find printed words and phrases that reflect your desires, you should only use those words that feel right for you. When you feel good about the words and phrases on your Vision Board, it means that those things are a part of your divine destiny. A friend who used her Vision Board to attract the perfect boyfriend, posted statements such as "THE LOVE THAT IS MINE NOW COMES TO ME UNDER DIVINE GUIDANCE, IN PERFECT WAYS AND IN PERFECT TIMING" and "I AM HAPPILY IN LOVE WITH A MAN WHO IS PATIENT, KIND, CARING AND COMMITTED TO ME." She met the man of her dreams after six months of commitment to the Law of Attraction. Today she is happily married to him.

As you prioritize your intentions, you might want to create more than one Vision Board to reflect the various areas of life that you want to transform through the creative power of intention. A successful writer in Los Angeles has three vision boards: one for romance, one for her writing career, and one for health and fitness. Her "Love and Romance" Vision Board hangs near her mirror so that she will be reminded to focus on manifesting romance while getting dressed in the morning. Her "Health and Fitness" Vision Board is posted in front of her treadmill so that she can focus on the feelings and images of vibrant health while exercising, and her "Very Successful Writer" Vision Board hangs above her desk so that she will be inspired to focus on professional goals while writing each day.

The fastest way to manifest with a Vision Board is to focus on it at least three times per day, but more often if time permits. For five minutes, focus on the words and images on your board while imagining the feelings that you would feel if your desire was your reality. If your images and words reflect the desire for romance, then you should imagine going on a date with your partner while feeling the joy and fulfillment that you would actually feel if you were in a loving relationship. If you want more money, for example, you should focus on the images that remind you of wealth; as you do so, you should imagine how you would feel to have lots of money to spend, save, and to buy the things you desire. As you do this, you might want to use the Intention Statement, "MY INTENTION IS TO BE FINANCIALLY PROSPEROUS SO THAT I CAN BUY ANYTHING I NEED OR WANT." If you have a Vision Board for vacation and travel, then you should imagine the feelings that you would experience if you were boarding a plane to an exotic destination. For example, as you focus on images of Paris, Rome or Hong Kong, you might want to use the Intention Statement, "MY INTENTION IS TO HAVE THE MONEY

...ORTUNITIES TO TRAVEL THE WORLD IN STYLE AND COMFORT." *The key to making your Vision Board work is to give attention to your intention on a regular basis.*

ADVANCED LAW OF ATTRACTION TECHNIQUE #3: EMOTIONAL VISUALIZATION

The late Neville Goddard is probably the most famous author to write about the creative power of imagination. Although he died decades before the Law of Attraction was a household topic, he wrote numerous books in which he explained how the human imagination can be used to influence events in the physical world. Neville Goddard's books, lectures and television appearances were very popular because many of his students had successfully used their imagination to manifest homes, jobs, health, money, and other wonderful things. Prior to the introduction of his unique approach, it was a common practice to visualize without using emotions, but Neville stressed that feeling-based imaginary scenes were required to stir up the belief and expectancy that precedes manifestation. As a result, the author of this book refers to this practice as Emotional Visualization, which is a fusion of creative visualization and emotions.

Prior to the teachings of Neville Goddard, scientists around the world were slowly becoming aware of the fact that human consciousness had the power to affect subatomic particles in the physical world. In 1909, Geoffrey Ingram Taylor, a British physicist, carried out the famous "double-slit" laboratory experiment in which he proved that the mere presence of people in the room (that is, their collective consciousness) affected the manner in which quantum particles were behaving. Nearly 90 years later, scientists at the Weizmann Institute of Science in Israel repeated the famous Taylor experiment. Not only did they confirm that the physical world is affected by human awareness or being watched, but they also discovered that the greater the amount of watching, the greater the influence on what actually takes place. In other words, the more focused attention we give our intentions, the faster will they manifest through the dynamic power of thought. Each time we visualize our desires with focus and emotion we set into motion the quantum mechanism that has the power to manifest our desires.

HOW TO USE EMOTIONAL VISUALIZATION

In order to use this powerful manifestation tool effectively, you should first warm up by thinking about something that you have enjoyed in the past, such as eating your favorite meal, spending time with a loved one, or going for a walk along the beach. If you choose to warm up by imagining your favorite meal, then spend five minutes imagining all the sensations, smells and tastes that you would experience if you were actually eating that meal. How does it taste? What does it smell like? What emotions do you feel as you imagine eating your meal? After a short warm-up session you will be better prepared to use Emotional Visualization effectively because your senses, emotions, and feelings will have been awakened. A friend from New York City always begins his exercise by performing a warm-up session in which he imagines running in the New York City Marathon. For five minutes, he imagines the sights, feelings and sensations that he would experience as a runner in the marathon. He also imagines seeing his friends and family members along the route cheering for him, and he feels the rush of emotion as he imagines the excitement of finishing the marathon. This short, yet powerful warm-up session prepares his mind to visualize the important things he wants to manifest. His commitment to Emotional Visualization has allowed him to create a lucrative business, acquire two Brownstone buildings in Manhattan, and save a considerable amount of money. He is living the life of his dreams because he was committed to using the tools of manifestation on a daily basis.

THREE EMOTIONAL VISUALIZATION EXERCISES

The purpose of the following exercises is to provide a practical example of how this manifestation tool should be used. These exercises will help you attract money, success, a loving relationship, or anything that you can make a part of your beliefs and feelings. They serve as basic outlines, so you may change them as you see fit. You might, for example, decide to add a lot of imagined dialogue to your exercises. On the other hand, you might feel better using less imagined dialogue and more vivid images during these exercises. The key to effective Emotional Visualization is to incorporate scenes and dialogue that encourage you to feel positive and expectant. There is a link between your feelings of expectancy and the time it takes for a manifestation to appear. If you can create and maintain a strong feeling of expectation, then your manifestation is guaranteed to show up.

EMOTIONAL VISUALIZATION EXERCISE #1: HOW TO USE EMOTIONAL VISUALIZATION FOR MONEY

Once you have completed a warm-up session to awaken your senses, you should imagine how you would feel to have an abundance of money for your pleasure. How would you feel to have lots of money in your wallet all the time? How would you feel if you had three hundred dollars to spend every day of your life? Try to capture the feeling of this reality, and then imagine doing the things you would do if you had lots of money to enjoy. If having lots of money means getting your car detailed once a week, then take an imaginary trip to the car wash and imagine how you would feel to have more than enough money to do this all the time. If living an abundant life means that you can eat at your favorite restaurant as often as you like, then take an imaginary trip to that restaurant, order your favorite meal, and then feel the satisfaction that you would feel if you always had more than enough money to do this whenever you want. If your imagination takes you into a department store, then imagine telling the clerk that you will pay cash for your items, and then feel the satisfaction of paying for everything in cash. Mentally hear your friends praise your prosperity, and then imagine saying to them, "Yes, I am very prosperous. I always have lots of money." As you imagine how you would feel to have lots of spending money, you might want to use an Intention Statement such as: MY INTENTION IS TO ALWAYS HAVE LOTS OF SPENDING MONEY SO THAT I CAN BUY ANYTHING AND EVERYTHING I WANT. As you use your imagination to create your desired reality do not rely on logic by trying to imagine where the money will come from. Logic does not exist in the realm of manifestation. Your manifestation is guaranteed to show up once you capture and maintain the feeling of having your desire.

EMOTIONAL VISUALIZATION EXERCISE #2: HOW TO USE EMOTIONAL VISUALIZATION FOR MATERIAL POSSESSIONS

Once you have completed a warm-up session to awaken your senses, you will be ready to begin the process of manifesting your desires. Do you want a new computer or a new television? You might even want to manifest a piano or the dream car you have always wanted. Once you know exactly what you want, you can imagine it into manifestation through the creative power of your thoughts and feelings. If you want a car, for example, you should capture the feeling that you would feel if you owned that particular car. Would a new car give you comfort and peace of mind? If so, then focus on these positive feelings as you take an imaginary drive in your new car. Imagine that your friends are complementing the car. Respond to them by mentally saying, "Thank you. I am so happy to have the car of my dreams." If you want a new home, for example, spend time thinking about what your life would be like in that home. How would you feel to come home to your new house each day after work? Would you feel happy and content? If so, try to capture those feelings and maintain them as you imagine yourself walking through your new home, going from room to room, and then relaxing in the family room. As you imagine how you would feel to have the home of your dreams, you might want to use an Intention Statement such as: MY INTENTION IS TO MANIFEST THE HOME OF MY DREAMS THAT IS BEAUTIFUL, COMFORTABLE, AND PERFECT FOR ME IN EVERY WAY. Do not rely on logic to imagine where the money and opportunities will come from to make this intention a reality. The manifestation will take place as long as you persist in imagining with feeling, clarity and expectation.

EMOTIONAL VISUALIZATION EXERCISE #3: HOW TO USE EMOTIONAL VISUALIZATION FOR LOVE

Once you have performed a warm-up session to awaken your senses, you will be ready to use Emotional Visualization to manifest a loving relationship with the person who is right for you. Do you enjoy long, romantic walks with a loved one? Does the thought of traveling abroad with a partner give you joy and fulfillment? Search your feelings and then spend time imagining scenes that encourage you and offer you hope. If you enjoy romantic walks, then imagine holding hands with your lover while walking along the beach or through a park. How does this relationship make you feel? Are you happy, fulfilled and content? If so, capture these positive feelings and maintain them as you perform this exercise. Imagine caressing your lover and then imagine how a kiss would make you feel. Add tones of reality to this exercise by imagining friends and family members complementing your relationship. Respond to them by mentally saying, "Thank you. I am so happy to have found the partner of my dreams." As you imagine how you would feel to be in a romantic relationship, you might want to use an Intention Statement such as: MY INTENTION IS TO FALL IN LOVE WITH SOMEONE WHO IS KIND, ROMANTIC AND A PERFECT MATCH FOR ME. Once again, do not rely on logic to imagine how this union will take place. There are a million ways in which your perfect partner can show up. Your job is not to determine how it will happen, but to know what you want and then feel the reality of being in love so that the Universal Law can deliver your desire.

ADVANCED LAW OF ATTRACTION TECHNIQUE #4: HOW TO USE MIRROR WORK

Mirror Work is a powerful transformative tool that is easy to use and very effective. The purpose of Mirror Work is to allow yourself to attract the things you want. No matter how much you want a particular thing, you will not manifest it unless you mentally and emotionally allow it to come into your life. For example, my friend Jon wanted to be prosperous, but he did not feel that he deserved to have lots of money. I asked where his limited feelings originated, and he responded by saying that he was brought up by parents who struggled with money. To make matters worse, they often argued about finances, so Jon's earliest thoughts and feelings about money were rooted in lack, limitation, and frustration. As he got older, he attracted events and circumstances that matched his negative feelings and expectations about money. By the time he was in his mid-thirties, he was ready for a major mental transformation, so I suggested that he implement a Law of Attraction action plan that included the use of Mirror Work twice a day.

Mirror Work was first introduced to readers around the world in a book titled THE MAGIC OF BELIEVING by Claude Bristol. In it, the author explains how readers can release their inner greatness and inspire themselves to positive action through the use of this dynamic tool. Although the book was first released in 1948, it is still in publication today. In fact, many business professionals, millionaires, and celebrities attribute their success to the ideas conveyed in this book. It has even been documented that Phyllis Diller and Liberace attributed their professional success to this book, which contains a lot of useful information about positive thinking, mental imagery, and mirror work. In recent times, Louise Hay has taught millions of her readers that Mirror Work leads to clarity, focus, spiritual healing, and transformation.

The good thing about Mirror Work is that it can be done easily and effectively within a few minutes per day. All that is required is privacy, a mirror, and the willingness to perform this simple exercise twice a day, once in the morning and again in the evening. Some people enjoy doing Mirror Work in their bathroom or in their bedroom. My friend Jon was in the habit of doing his Mirror Work in the bathroom after brushing his teeth in the morning and again after dinner. His ritual was to relax in front of the mirror and then speak to his reflection. Looking into his eyes, he would say, "Jon, I know that you want to have more money to enjoy the finer things in life. You want more money for a better car, for savings and for travel. I want you to know that I allow you to have all the money and opportunities you desire. I acknowledge the fact that you once believed in lack and limitation, but I now allow you to experience more opportunities, abundance and prosperity through the Law of Attraction. I want you to prosper and I allow you to prosper now." Jon's Allowing Statement is a very good example of effective Mirror Work. Feel free to use his example, but compose your Allowing Statement with words and phrases that meet your particular needs and feelings.

Jon said that his Mirror Work was challenging at first because he felt uneasy about looking into his eyes in the mirror and speaking to his reflection, but over time the exercise became easier and more enjoyable. In addition, the exercise helped him break through many of the financial barriers that held him back in the past. Within a few months, his financial life turned around because he got a promotion at work, he started saving money, and he began to attract more opportunities and prosperity from expected and unexpected avenues of expression.

"Most of all," Jon said one evening during a phone call, "I started feeling better about money. My feelings and expectations changed, so good things started happening as a result." Jon went on to say that he continues to use Mirror Work and the other tools of manifestation on a daily basis. He now has more money than ever before, and he has even used Mirror Work to allow himself to attract a loving relationship with a woman who has similar spiritual interests.

ADVANCED LAW OF ATTRACTION TECHNIQUE #5: HOW TO USE A BELIEF STATEMENT

The purpose of a Belief Statement is to help you focus on your beliefs in order to accelerate the manifestation process. When used properly, a Belief Statement will increase your positive feelings and expectation, which are essential elements of the manifestation process. Many people who have incorporated a Belief Statement into their Law of Attraction action plan have experienced increased income, greater opportunities, and a positive outlook on life within a short amount of time. The best part about using a Belief Statement is that it is easy to use and can help you feel positive, focused and expectant immediately.

The following statements are good examples of effective Belief Statements:

1) I believe that good things can happen to me.
2) I believe that I can be prosperous.
3) I believe that I can have lots of money.
4) I believe that I can fall in love with someone who is perfect for me.

The key to success with a Belief Statement is to use statements that feel true to you. If a Belief Statement does not feel true, then you cannot expect it to increase your faith in the manifestation process, so take the time to search your feelings for words and ideas that make you feel good. For best results, your Belief Statement should be short, to the point, and it should accurately reflect your feelings. Some people affirm their Belief Statement as they drive to work or while taking a shower. The good thing about a Belief Statement is that it can be used in place of affirmations for those people who do not enjoy repeating affirmations. For example, a friend from Chicago did not enjoy repeating affirmations because they did not arouse his interest, but he enjoyed the way he felt when he used his Belief Statement throughout the day. He said that his Belief Statement made him feel positive, expectant and enthusiastic because it encouraged him to focus on the way he felt about his intentions. Through his daily commitment to the Law of Attraction, he manifested his desire for a satisfying, well-paying job within a relatively short amount of time.

Belief Statements are dynamic and can be changed as your beliefs evolve. For example, if you don't feel comfortable saying "I believe that good things can happen to me", then you should start with the statement, "I want to believe that good things can happen to me" or "I want to believe that I can have lots of money." As you persist in using the tools of manifestation on a daily basis, your beliefs and feelings will evolve, and eventually you will feel comfortable affirming that good things can happen to you. When this shift takes place, you will be in the metaphysical mindset to manifest your desires. Neville Goddard conveyed the idea best when he wrote that "Feeling Is The Secret" to manifestation. If you feel it, then you can have it.

Begin now by writing one or two Belief Statements that you can use throughout the day. Feel free to use the statements that are provided, but keep in mind that the words you write are the most powerful Belief Statements you can use because they reflect your personal thoughts and feelings. Once you have written a few Belief Statements that make you feel good, write them on a small card so that you will be reminded to repeat them throughout the day.

PART 2: Manifesting Desires - Interviews with people who have manifested desires with the Law of Attraction

LUCY'S LAW OF ATTRACTION ACTION PLAN

I met Lucy at the Church of Religious Science in Los Angeles many years ago. Since then, we have kept in touch through phone calls and the occasional lunch date. Throughout the years, Lucy has experienced a great amount of success with the Law of Attraction, but her success did not manifest until she learned to overcome limited thinking by changing her thoughts, feelings and expectations about money. As a child she was brought up to believe that money was scarce and that financial struggles were the norm. As a result, she often struggled with money and rarely had extra cash after her monthly bills were paid. In short, her thoughts, feelings and expectations were keeping her stuck in a life characterized by lack and limitation. Once she learned about the creative power of her thoughts and feelings, she began the spiritual work that would place her on the path to success and prosperity. As she used the tools of manifestation on a daily basis, she gradually expanded her limited thoughts, feelings and expectations to reflect a prosperous lifestyle. Six months after implementing her Law of Attraction action plan, she left an unsatisfying job as a file clerk, and started selling real estate shortly after earning her state license. During her first year as a real estate agent, she earned twice her former income, and the following year she earned much more than that.

During lunch one afternoon, Lisa revealed her daily ritual to me, "I always start the day with my Intention Statement, which I have printed on a laminated card. First thing in the morning I affirm: MY INTENTION IS TO THRIVE IN THE REAL ESTATE BUSINESS BY CLOSING LOTS OF DEALS, GETTING GOOD LISTINGS, AND WORKING WITH QUALIFIED CLIENTS." Her laminated card sits on her desk as a reminder to focus on her intentions regularly. Throughout the day, she feelingly repeats her Intention Statement as often as possible. At night, she repeats it before going to bed, and the following morning this powerful ritual begins again. In addition to using her Intention Statement, she spends a few minutes in the morning, afternoon and evening vividly imagining how she would feel to live the life of her dreams. She said that her Emotional Visualization exercises helped her feel more comfortable with the money and success she desired, which made it much easier for her to prosper. She went on to explain, "Some people think that using their imagination is difficult, but it's not. You become quiet, close your eyes and then imagine what you would like to experience with feeling and emotion. I imagine making lots of sales at work, seeing my clients sign sales documents, and I feel the reality of big commission checks in my hands. I always feel wonderful and expectant when I finish my exercises."

Lucy was kind enough to provide some practical information about Emotional Visualization. According to her, the following guidelines should be considered when using this powerful manifestation tool:

1) Find a quiet place where you can be alone for a few minutes each day. You can use your bedroom, your car, or any place where you can concentrate undisturbed for a while.

2) Relax, close your eyes, and then imagine what your desired life would be like and feel like. Imagine how you would feel to own the car of your dreams, work at your dream job, or to have a fulfilling relationship with someone who is a perfect match for you. Using emotions, actions and dialogue, create mental movies in which you do the things that you would do if your dreams were your reality. If images help you imagine more vividly, then you should use a Vision Board to help you imagine the things you want to make a part of your life.

3) Visualize twice per day, ten minutes each time; once in the morning to set the tone of your day, and again in the evening to program your subconscious mind prior to sleep. The amount of time you spend is not as important as the quality of time you spend incorporating feelings of reality into your exercises. If you can feel good and expectant after ten minutes of Emotional Visualization, then your exercise has been a success.

4) If you experience resistance or have a difficult time feeling the reality of your desires, then start by imagining something smaller until you feel more comfortable about your intention. Once you feel more comfortable, you should take it up a notch by imagining something larger. For example, if you have a difficult time feeling the reality of $25,000.00 in your bank account, then experiment with how $10,000.00 would make you feel. As you perform this exercise each day, your beliefs will evolve and you will gradually feel better about these exercises.

5) Don't expect to become a pro after the first few weeks, so be patient with yourself. Commit to your exercises by imagining with focus and emotion. Eventually your expectation will increase, and when this happens your desires will begin to show up in your life.

Lucy is now prospering more than ever as a result of her Law of Attraction action plan. Although she maintains a busy work schedule, she continues to use the tools of manifestation on a daily basis. As a result of her commitment to the Law of Attraction, she now takes overseas vacations, drives her dream car, and has more money than she can spend. She owes her success to the fact that she has added the necessary ingredient of action to the Law of Attraction.

JACOB'S LAW OF ATTRACTION ACTION PLAN

I met Jacob at a Law of Attraction workshop in Los Angeles, California. Throughout the years we have attended a number of spiritual workshops and lectures throughout Southern California. Jacob now lives in New York City where he runs a café. He said that his dream was to move to Manhattan ever since his first trip to the Big Apple during the summer of 2004. Feeling that he was destined to live in New York City, he began making plans to relocate there while still living in Los Angeles. At that time, there was no evidence to suggest that it was possible for him to relocate to New York City. He had very little savings and no experience operating a business, but he had worked in various cafes throughout Southern California, and he possessed a profound desire that he thought about constantly. Although negative thinking sometimes hindered his progress, he spent time affirming and visualizing a new, exciting life in New York City. In an e-mail message to me, Jacob explained that he always started each morning by repeating his Intention Statement: "MY INTENTION IS TO THRIVE IN LIFE AND BUSINESS IN NEW YORK CITY." Being familiar with the tremendous power of repetition, he repeated his Intention Statement several times throughout the day as he went about his busy schedule. Jacob also used affirmations for fifteen minutes per day. His favorite affirmation was: "I LOVE THE THOUGHT OF LIVING AND THRIVING IN NEW YORK CITY. I AM NOW IN THE

PROCESS OF RELOCATING THERE THROUGH THE LAW OF ATTRACTION." I asked Jacob why he chose that particular affirmation, and his response was enlightening: "If I affirmed that I was living in New York while I was still in Los Angeles, the affirmation would have felt untrue, so I affirmed that I loved the thought of living in New York City. Since it was true that I was in the process of relocating there, this affirmation made me feel positive and expectant."

I agreed with Jacob's approach because affirmations must arouse good feelings in order to work effectively. We cannot expect to create positive experiences if we use an affirmation that does not feel good when repeating it. Affirmations that arouse expectant feelings are powerful tools of manifestation; we will have better results by saying "I am now in the process of manifesting lots of money with the Law of Attraction" than by affirming "I am rich and prosperous" if we do not feel rich and prosperous. We always create circumstances that match our predominant feelings and expectations.

During a recent trip to New York City I made plans to have coffee with Jacob near his apartment in the West Village, so we agreed on Starbucks across from Sheridan Square. We met on the morning of October 31st, and I could already sense the festive Halloween spirit in the chilly morning air. In fact, a few people dressed in costumes were already stopping by for their morning coffee before work. Fortunately, I did not have to wait long for Jacob, who crossed 7th Avenue and made his way into the coffee shop to greet me.

After catching up on personal matters, I asked Jacob to share his insights and manifestation techniques for this book. I wanted to know what he did each day to manifest his desires. Without missing a beat, he said that his success was a result of the fact that he used the tools of manifestation each day. "I would not have succeeded," he said with sincerity, "if I did not visualize and affirm my success every day. I would imagine the excitement that I would feel while riding the subway and taking cabs all over the city, and I felt the fall breeze on my face as I walked up and down the avenues. I also imagined how I would feel to run a successful café in the city. Mentally, I greeted customers, chatted with employees, and I visualized money filling my cash register." Jacob said that he used Emotional Visualization for months before booking his flight to JFK Airport. In addition to using the tools of manifestation, he spent time dealing with his negative thinking. He admitted to engaging in bitter and resentful thoughts at times, especially toward a former co-worker who still owed him money. After taking a sip of coffee, Jacob explained, "I knew that in order to use the Law of Attraction successfully I would have to clean up my mental and emotional clutter by giving up bitterness and resentment, so I stopped replaying negative memories once and for all." Once he released the mental clutter, he felt better and more in alignment with the Universal Law, which is characterized by order, balance, and harmony. He admitted that it was not easy at first, but he persisted until he gave up all forms of negative thinking, including anger, sarcasm, jealousy, and gossip. He realized that his negative thoughts had the power to block manifestations because all prolonged thoughts and feelings are creative and will eventually show up as events and circumstances in life.

After a few months of commitment to his Law of attraction action plan, opportunities unfolded that allowed him to relocate to New York City. With some money in the bank and a check from his father, Jacob flew to New York where he continued using the tools of manifestation daily. Although he had no trouble finding a job and a place to live, his dreams began to take form when a co-worker just happened to mention her desire to open a café. She had the necessary start-up money and the perfect location in mind, but little of the initiative and creativity that Jacob naturally possessed. Jacob took immediate interest in his co-worker's vision and saw it as a positive sign that his dream could soon become a reality, so they discussed the possibilities, drew up a business plan, and opened a small café in the city. Within a year of arriving in New York, Jacob was living the life that he had imagined while in Los Angeles. He credits his dedication to the Law of Attraction for his success, and believes that his creative marketing and advertising ideas came as a result of imagining success daily. As a result of his intentions, his mind was flooded with creative ideas and unique strategies that helped his business take off quickly and successfully.

As the coffee warmed us, I asked Jacob if he ever doubted his ability to manifest his dreams. He replied by saying that he had faith in the manifestation process because he knew a number of people who had successfully manifested desires with the Law of Attraction, but his biggest challenge was creating a Law of Attraction action plan that was easy to use each day. At first he attempted to use Emotional Visualization for an hour per day, but soon realized that an hour was not always possible considering his busy schedule, so he cut back to twenty minutes per day. As a result of his Emotional Visualization exercises, he became comfortable with his dream of living and thriving in New York City. As he continued to use the tools of manifestation to enlarge his beliefs and expectations, the Universal Law was putting all the pieces in order so that he would make the right choices and meet the right people to make his dreams come true.

Before we finished our coffee and walked back out into the cold morning air, Jacob was kind enough to reveal some information about his manifestation technique. He said that he did the following things each day as part of his Law of Attraction action plan:

1) He started each day with his Intention Statement. He said that it kept him motivated and focused on manifesting his desires.

2) In order to feel the reality of his desires, he used Emotional Visualization for twenty minutes per day. Jacob said that his goals were achieved because he used Emotional

Visualization each day even when he did not feel inspired. He claims that it was this "mental rehearsal" that attracted the events, circumstances, and opportunities that made his dreams a reality.

3) He repeated three different affirmations before and after his Emotional Visualization exercises. I asked why he limited his spoken affirmations to three, and he replied by saying that too many affirmations scattered his attention.

4) He used a Vision Board to help him focus on his desires. His Vision Board featured images of money, a busy restaurant scene, and other things that reminded him of his intention to live and thrive in New York City. His board also contained phrases such as "I AM SUCCESSFUL AND PROSPEROUS IN EVERYTHING I DO" and "ALL MY PLANS, IDEAS AND INTENTIONS RESULT IN SUCCESS." He focused on his Vision Board twice a day for five minutes each time.

5) Twice a day, once in the morning and again in the evening, Jacob repeated his Allowing Statement as he stood before a mirror. He would take a minute to relax, and then he would look into his reflection and say, "Jacob, I know that you want to live and thrive in New York City. This has been your dream for many years. I want you to know that you deserve to live the life of your dreams. In fact, you were destined to be prosperous, successful and happy. I now allow you to experience the life of your dreams. I know that moving to a new city might be frightening, but you will succeed because living and thriving in New York City is your destiny." Jacob said that his Allowing Statement helped him feel better about achieving his dream. In addition, it helped him move past the doubt about whether or not he was making the right decision to pack up and leave. As he continued to use Mirror Work each day, he began to feel better about his intention

and more convinced that his success was guaranteed. As he felt better about success, he began to attract more success.

Jacob is now more successful than ever in life and business. He continues to operate a cafe and is in the process of opening a diner in Brooklyn. He also continues to use the tools of manifestation on a daily basis to manifest additional desires.

Before concluding the interview I asked Jacob if he thought that he could have accomplished his success without using the Law of Attraction. He replied by saying, "Everything that brought me to New York City is a result of the mental blueprint that I created while living in Los Angeles. I created the blueprint in my thoughts and feelings, and the Universal Law prepared the way and opened doors for me."

LISA'S LAW OF ATTRACTION ACTION PLAN

Lisa is a close friend whom I met during a workshop at the Bodhi Tree Book Store in West Hollywood, California. Unfortunately, The Bodhi Tree is now closed, but for over forty years it was a bustling outlet filled with countless books, tapes, CDs, and other Spiritual and New Thought materials. It was the largest and most popular metaphysical book store on the West Coast of the United States. The Bodhi Tree is greatly missed by the thousands of people who stopped by regularly to attend workshops or to peruse the magazines, spiritual classics, and new releases while sampling the herbal tea that was freely provided. I found some of my most treasured books in the used book branch located in a small building behind the main store.

One particular evening during the fall of 2009 I received a phone call from Lisa, who wanted to learn how to speed up her manifestations. Although she had manifested some small intentions with the Law of Attraction, she wanted to understand the art of manifestation more thoroughly so that she could use it to get the job she desperately needed. In fact, she was becoming more desperate with each passing week because payments on her student loans would soon be due. At that particular time in America, a profound financial recession was affecting millions of people throughout the country. Many companies were downsizing, layoff notices were being printed, and the job market was gloomy. As a result, Lisa had spent a year desperately searching for a job after finishing grad school with a Master's Degree of Business Administration.

That evening on the phone I explained to Lisa that her feelings of desperation would always work against her by attracting more events and circumstances to feel desperate about. Since the Law of Attraction responds to positive and negative feelings, it will produce positive or negative events to match our dominant feelings. As a result of our conversation, Lisa realized that the key to her success lay in her ability to change her feelings and expectations by using the tools of manifestation each day. In order to do so, I suggested that she implement a Law of Attraction action plan to eliminate desperate feelings and then replace them with faith and expectation.

I told Lisa to do the following:

1) Create an Intention Statement that is short, to the point, and make sure it feels good when repeating it. Once you have created your statement, begin each day by repeating it feelingly and thoughtfully. As you repeat it, imagine yourself having and doing the things you desire. You should repeat your Intention Statement at least three times per day, but up to a dozen times per day if time permits.

2) Write three to five affirmations that make you feel positive and expectant when repeating them. You can find lots of affirmations in books and on websites, but the affirmations that you

create are the most powerful statements to use because they reflect your particular thoughts, feelings and expectations. Also, pay attention to how certain words make you feel. For example, if the words ABUNDANCE and FANTASTIC make you feel good, then you should consider using these words in your affirmations.

3) Decide what you want to focus on during your Emotional Visualization exercises. If you want a new job, for example, you should create imaginary scenes in which you are happily working at that job, interacting with coworkers, and then imagine the excitement that you would feel when cashing your paycheck. You may want to use dialogue in these scenes by imagining that your friends are congratulating you on finding the perfect job. The more tones of reality you add to these Emotional Visualization exercises, the more powerful your intention becomes. Use three or four mental scenes that make you feel positive and expectant. For these imaginary exercises, use imagined dialogue, imagined actions, feelings and as many tones of reality as you can imagine.

4) Create a Belief Statement to build faith and expectancy throughout the day. Your Belief Statement should be short, to the point, and it should reflect the way you feel about your desires and your ability to manifest them. For example, your Belief Statement might be, "I believe that I am destined to be prosperous, successful and happy. If others have manifested success with the Law of Attraction, so can I!" If you experience emotional resistance and doubt then you should use Mirror Work and an Allowing Statement to move past the negative beliefs that sometimes hinder success.

Lisa followed my advice. During a phone call one afternoon she said, "Several times during the day I repeated my Intention Statement, which was: "MY INTENTION IS TO HAVE A WONDERFUL JOB THAT MAKES ME HAPPY, UTILIZES MY TALENTS, AND PAYS

ME WELL." Lisa also reported using Emotional Visualization each day. Using emotion and tones of reality, she would imagine arriving at her new job, sitting at her desk, and then she would carry on imaginary conversations with coworkers. She would feelingly imagine what she would do if she had the job of her dreams, and then she would express gratitude for her fulfilled desire. When I asked Lisa how long she used Emotional Visualization each day, she responded, "I did it three times a day for ten minutes, but I increased these sessions if I had extra time during the day. I always added emotion to these exercises, and I even did them when I did not feel inspired. I was persistent and tried to be as positive as possible at all times."

Lisa said that nothing out of the ordinary happened at first. For some time, she even doubted her ability to manifest success because of past experience in the job market, but she persisted knowing that the Universal Law would respond to her thoughts and feelings of success. In addition to using an Intention Statement throughout the day, she used spoken affirmations to create and maintain positive, expectant feelings. Her favorite affirmation was: "I LOVE HAVING LOTS OF MONEY, AND IT NOW RUSHES INTO MY LIFE IN OVERFLOWING ABUNDANCE." I asked Lisa to explain how this particular affirmation made her feel, and she replied by saying that the idea of money rushing into her life made her feel excited and expectant. The word OVERFLOWING encouraged her to imagine a river of money flowing into her life. She also said that she always spoke affirmations for 15 to 20 minutes per day depending upon how much free time she had.

Eventually Lisa began feeling more positive and expectant because of the change that was taking place within her. She realized that her expectation had increased because she was taking time each day to affirm and visualize her desired reality. She understood that the more expectant we feel, the faster will we manifest our intentions.

Not long after committing to her Law of Attraction action plan, Lisa said that doors started opening for her in the form of job interviews, callbacks, and requests for her resume. As she continued to use the tools of manifestation daily, her feelings began to shift from desperation to hope and expectation. One afternoon she received an e-mail requesting an interview from the human resources manager of a local hospital. A week later she was scheduled for an interview, and two weeks after that she was offered a job working in the finance section of a large medical center in Los Angeles. A month after starting the job, Lisa sent me a card that read, "I am so happy that you encouraged me to persist with the Law of Attraction. Now I can see that the Universe was lining up all my opportunities while I was repeating my Intention Statement, using affirmations and doing my Emotional Visualization exercises each day. Thank you for showing me that this power works if you work it!"

As of this writing Lisa still works for the hospital, but she has been promoted to assistant manager of the budget unit. In addition, she continues to use Emotional Visualization and spoken affirmations to maintain positivity and expectancy in her affairs. She is now enjoying the life of her dreams because she was committed to using the tools of manifestation every day until her desires became her reality.

PART 3: Manifesting Love and Relationships - Interviews with people who have manifested love and relationships with the Law of Attraction

STEPHANIE'S LAW OF ATTRACTION ACTION PLAN

Stephanie was my classmate in junior college many years ago. We had an instant rapport because of our similar interest in spiritual books and New Age workshops. Although we had lost touch for many years after earning our associates degrees, we bumped into each other at a metaphysical book store in Los Angeles during the spring of 2014. She was shopping for a book about manifesting love and relationships, so I mentioned some titles that I considered worth reading. I also mentioned that I knew a number of people who had attracted loving relationships with the Law of Attraction, so she was naturally interested in learning what they did each day to manifest love and romance.

Stephanie had been out of the dating scene for a number of years. Her last relationship ended in a bitter breakup because she and her boyfriend could not agree on important issues, but she was now ready to establish a quality relationship with someone who shared her dreams, which included marriage and a family. She was also ready to follow a Law of Attraction action plan to manifest her desires as soon as possible. As a result, I told her to set aside time each day to use an Intention Statement, spoken affirmations and Emotional Visualization. Since she enjoyed repeating affirmations, I suggested that she focus most of her energy on spoken affirmations and an Intention Statement, but I urged her to add dialogue to her Emotional Visualization exercises to feel more empowered when using this powerful tool. As a result of my encouragement, Stephanie implemented a Law of Attraction action plan to manifest her desires. In fact, she was so serious about success that by the following day she had written an Intention Statement and a number of spoken affirmations.

About six weeks after our chance meeting at the book store, I got a call from Stephanie asking to meet so that she could share some good news with me. The following day we met at a coffee shop near her home in West Los Angeles. She was excited to see me again, but she was even more excited to tell me about her progress with the Law of Attraction. It turns out that she met a parcel delivery man at her job. He caught her attention quickly because he remembered her name and always asked how she was doing. A few weeks after meeting him, he asked her out on a date, and she accepted. By the time we met for coffee, she had already been on a number of dates with Sam.

    Naturally, I was curious to hear details about Stephanie's manifestation exercises, so I asked her to explain what she thought about and imagined while using Emotional Visualization. She responded by saying that she added a lot of positive emotions and dialogue so that her imaginary scenes would take on the feeling of reality. After a warm up session, she would imagine how she would feel to be on a date with her boyfriend. She would imagine getting into his car, kissing him, and driving to the movies while they chatted about the events of the day. She would even imagine her boyfriend saying that he loved her, and she would respond with: "I love you, too." She would then imagine how she would feel to hold his hand while entering the theater, and then she would imagine how she would feel to cuddle next to him during the film. Sometimes she would imagine her boyfriend taking her to a trendy restaurant in Culver City or to a concert at the Hollywood Bowl. Although she frequently imagined going to dinner and the movies, she would occasionally focus on different scenes to keep her exercises interesting. She always enjoyed amusement parks, so she would often imagine how she would feel to visit Disneyland with her boyfriend. No matter which scene she used during her Emotional Visualization exercises, she always incorporated dialogue and feelings.

    Stephanie said that spoken affirmations made her feel positive and expectant. She believes that words are creative because they can make a person feel hopeful or gloomy depending on the nature of the words used. When I asked if she thought that her Intention Statement helped speed up her manifestation, she replied by saying that the constant use of it kept her on track and focused on the manifestation of her desires. As a result of using it, she was constantly aware that all her words, thoughts and feelings were creating her reality.

Here is Stephanie's Law of Attraction Action Plan:

1) Each morning Stephanie repeated her Intention Statement, which was "MY INTENTION IS TO HAVE A LOVING, SUPPORTIVE, AND AWESOME RELATIONSHIP WITH A MAN WHO LOVES ME JUST AS I AM." Even though she had a busy schedule, she always made time to repeat her Intention Statement a number of times throughout the day. Sometimes she would repeat it while getting ready for work or while preparing meals. She even wrote her Intention Statement on a small card that she placed near her computer so that she would remember to repeat it each time she checked her e-mail.

2) Stephanie wrote a number of spoken affirmations that encouraged her to feel positive and expectant about manifesting the relationship she desired. Her favorite affirmation was, "I BELIEVE THAT I CAN EXPERIENCE LOVE AND ROMANCE RIGHT NOW. I SEE LOVE WHEREVER I GO, AND PERFECT LOVE NOW COMES TO ME IN PERFECT WAYS AND IN PERFECT TIMING."

3) Twice a day Stephanie used Emotional Visualization infused with dialogue. Initially, this exercise was challenging because she did not enjoy visualizing in the past, but I told her to begin her exercise with a warm up session to awaken her feelings and senses. Once her feelings and senses were awakened, she would be in the perfect mental state to use Emotional Visualization effectively. As a result, Stephanie would warm up by closing her eyes and replaying happy memories in her mind, such as hugging her grandfather, playing with her favorite childhood pet, or visiting Paris after graduating from high school. Stephanie admitted that she always felt better after a five minute warm up session. In fact, she eventually enjoyed using Emotional Visualization very much, and would often spend fifteen minutes, twice per day using this manifestation tool.

4) Because Stephanie enjoyed crafting, she cut out and posted colorful images on her Vision Board. She included pictures of couples walking together, laughing together and caressing. She also included statements on her Vision Board, such as "I AM IN LOVE WITH THE PERFECT MAN FOR ME and I AM IN A FULFILLING, LOVING RELATIONSHIP THAT IS FILLED WITH UNCONDITIONAL LOVE, TRUST, AND RESPECT."

Stephanie and Sam are now very much in love with one another. They continue to spend most of their free time together, and they even visit Disneyland as often as possible. Sam is a great guy who really enjoys spending time with Stephanie. I know this firsthand because the three of us had dinner one evening in Redondo Beach.

Not long after our dinner by the beach, I asked Stephanie if she had any particular insights about how she manifested the love of her life. Without hesitation she said, "I manifested the love I wanted because I used the Law of Attraction each day no matter what was happening in my life. I made no excuses about doing my daily exercises. I was persistent about using my Intention Statement, and I also set aside time for Emotional Visualization and affirmations. I knew that nothing would happen for me unless I added the necessary ingredient of action to the Law of Attraction."

MICHAEL'S LAW OF ATTRACTION ACTION PLAN

Michael was a member of my first Law of Attraction study group in Los Angeles many years ago. Twice a month, a group of people would meet at my apartment to study books such as THE DYNAMIC LAWS OF PROSPERITY by Catherine Ponder and THE POWER OF AWARENESS by Neville Goddard. After discussing the assigned reading, we would have a round table discussion in which we would share metaphysical insights and discuss our successes and challenges with the Law of Attraction. Although the group lasted two years, many of the core members still keep in touch to this day. In fact, throughout the years Michael and I have attended a number of metaphysical workshops at the various book stores and spiritual centers throughout Southern California.

Although Michael had always enjoyed an active social life and had many friends, he confessed to having a difficult time establishing romantic relationships with women. In the past, he dated a number of women who seemed perfect for him at first, but unfortunate circumstances often prevented the relationship from blossoming. Michael said that he was unlucky when it came to love, but I told him that luck had nothing to do with it because he possessed a lot of great relationship qualities, such as intelligence, sincerity, and honesty. "The problem," I said one evening during a phone call, "is the negative feelings that repel your desires. The good news is that you can use the Law of Attraction and the power of intention to change your thoughts, feelings, and the events of your life."

A few days after our telephone conversation, I met Michael for lunch at the San Pedro Fish Market to enjoy a tray of fried fish, shrimp, and garlic bread. As we enjoyed our meal overlooking the waterfront, we discussed a Law of Attraction action plan that would help him attract the love of his life. Although he had manifested money, trips and business opportunities with the Law of Attraction, he never used it to manifest a relationship, so he asked me to explain the importance of using an Intention Statement for the manifestation of his desires.

I explained that the persistent use of an Intention Statement would program his Reticular Activating System for success. The Reticular Activating System, also known as the RAS, is a tiny part of the human brain that serves as a filter between the conscious and the subconscious mind. In a nutshell, it's a goal-seeking mechanism that filters out important information for human awareness. "Your persistent thoughts and feelings," I explained to Michael, "tells your Reticular Activating System what is important to you and what you want to experience more of. As a result, it will respond by making you more aware of the things that are important to you. If your intention is to have more money, then your Reticular Activating System will constantly work to make you aware of money making opportunities and situations that will provide the opportunity to get what you desire." I continued by explaining that the Reticular Activating System has a major impact upon the success or failure of a person given the quality of information it receives from the conscious mind. For example, the optimistic person who speaks positive words always seems to attract positive experiences while the pessimistic person never seems to get a break in life. Success or failure in life depends upon our intentions and how effectively we use our Reticular Activating System.

"So," Michael responded, "my job is to repeat my Intention Statement, and then my Reticular Activating System will do the rest?"

"Yes," I told him, "but be sure to repeat your Intention Statement with interest. Don't just repeat it mechanically. Say it with interest, and eventually your intention will take root in your subconscious mind. When that happens, your RAS will switch to automatic, and your desired relationship will come much easier and faster."

Michael was also interested in learning how to make his spoken affirmations more enjoyable. He said that he enjoyed using Emotional Visualization, but he was concerned because affirmations did not stimulate his interest. I explained that sometimes men enjoy visualizing more than repeating affirmations because of the way men are emotionally wired. Men, for example, are more naturally stimulated by images than words. Because Michael enjoyed using Emotional Visualization, I suggested that he incorporate dialogue into his daily exercises to help him feel more comfortable using the spoken word as part of his Law of Attraction action plan. For example, I suggested that he imagine a two-way conversation with his desired girlfriend in which he would hear her say, "I love you." I told him to respond to her imaginary words with whatever words he would use if he had a girlfriend. I also suggested that he occasionally repeat his Intention Statement during his Emotional Visualization exercises. "Add words to your imaginary scenes," I said to Michael, "and what you imagine will manifest if you persist in feeling the reality of your desires."

As we enjoyed the meal, Michael asked me to outline a Law of Attraction action plan for his use, so I suggested that he do the following things each day:

1) Beginning each morning, thoughtfully repeat your Intention Statement throughout the day. Keep in mind that all your words are creative, so only speak positive words throughout the day. Keep your mind alert for words that make you feel good, and use those words regularly. Never gossip and never talk about your former experiences with relationships. If negativity or doubt enters your mind, shift your attention by focusing on what you desire and by repeating your Intention Statement to neutralize the negativity. If you continue to do this, your Reticular Activating System will switch to automatic and success will happen much faster for you.

2) Use Emotional Visualization at least twice per day, but more often if time permits. Find a quiet place in which to relax and then imagine how you would feel to have a satisfying relationship with a loving woman. How would you treat her? How would she make you feel? What would she say to you? Where would you take her? Do not limit yourself because of past experiences. It is very important to go where your feelings lead you, so you should imagine doing with her what you would do if she was a part of your life right now. Use feelings, words and all the tones of reality that you can add to your Emotional Visualization exercises. Even if

you do not enjoy repeating affirmations, you can make the most of the spoken word by speaking positive words throughout the day and by adding dialogue to your Emotional Visualization exercises.

3)   Pay attention to your feelings because the Universal Law speaks the language of feelings. If you sense a strong rapport with a woman, then you might consider inviting her out on a date, but if a person or a situation makes you feel uneasy, then do nothing. You are not required to date every woman you meet, so exercise wisdom and pay attention to your feelings. You will know if a situation is right for you because there will be no question in your mind when you meet the right person.

Michael was committed to using the tools of manifestation to attract his soulmate no matter how much time and effort was required. Although he was busy working a full-time job and attending evening classes at community college, he made time for his Intention Statement and Emotional Visualization exercises several times per day. Because he did not want to express any form of negativity that could cancel his positive intention, he paid close attention to every thought he entertained and every word that came out of his mouth. If he had nothing positive to say about a person or a situation, he said nothing.

Four months after implementing a Law of Attraction action plan, a coworker introduced Michael to a single woman named Sarah. After an enjoyable, impromptu coffee date at a local Starbucks, Michael asked Sarah out to dinner the following weekend. Throughout the following weeks Michael and Sarah enjoyed the company of one another as they became better acquainted and eventually made the decision to start a relationship. Michael later admitted that Sarah was a perfect match for him because they both shared a lot of interests, including music, travel and cultural exploration. When I asked Michael to share his feelings and insights about the manifestation process, he replied, "I think the Law of Attraction brought her into my life at the perfect time. I knew this relationship was the right one for me when, out of the blue, Sarah invited me to see an exhibit at the Los Angeles County Museum of Art. Months before I met her, my favorite Emotional Visualization exercise was to imagine how I would feel to enjoy the Los Angeles art scene with a girlfriend."

Michael and Sarah now live together and are making plans to be married.

PART 4: Common Denominators of Successful Manifestations

The people interviewed for this book had unique interests and intentions, but they shared a similar goal of manifesting their desires with the Law of Attraction. Lucy, for example, wanted more money and professional success while Jacob wanted to relocate to NYC to operate a successful business. Lisa was in the market for a satisfying career, which she manifested through the power of intention. Finally, Stephanie and Michael established an intention to manifest love with the Law of Attraction. Each of the interviewees understood the life-transforming power of intention, and they used it daily to manifest their desires. Although each interviewee had responsibilities to tend to each day, such as work and families, each individual spent time focusing on their Law of Attraction action plan. Instead of reading book after book about the Law of Attraction, they were dedicated to harnessing this creative power through their daily, committed action.

1) Lucy used the tools of manifestation on a daily basis. She repeated her Intention Statement several times per day, and twice per day she used Emotional Visualization to feel the reality of her desired success. Her Intention Statement was: MY INTENTION IS TO THRIVE IN THE REAL ESTATE BUSINESS BY CLOSING LOTS OF DEALS, GETTING GOOD LISTINGS,

AND WORKING WITH QUALIFIED CLIENTS. As she repeated her Intention Statement, she imagined closing lots of deals, seeing clients sign escrow paperwork, and she mentally experienced the excitement of having large commission checks in her hands. Through the creative power of intention and expectancy, she manifested her desires by earning much more money than she had ever earned in the past.

2) Months before Jacob manifested the means to make his dream a reality, he took time each day to repeat his Intention Statement, which was: "MY INTENTION IS TO THRIVE IN LIFE AND BUSINESS IN NEW YORK CITY." He always repeated his Intention Statement with interest and focus. In addition, he only used affirmations that made him feel good. His favorite affirmation was: "I LOVE THE THOUGHT OF LIVING AND THRIVING IN NEW YORK CITY. I AM NOW IN THE PROCESS OF RELOCATING THERE THROUGH THE LAW OF ATTRACTION." In addition, he often spent quality time using Emotional Visualization to experience the reality of his desires. During these exercises, he would mentally greet customers, carry on imaginary conversations with employees, and he would visualize lots of money filling his cash register. He would also imagine the joy he would experience knowing that every table of his cafe was filled with happy, satisfied customers. He always felt good during and after his Emotional Visualization exercises. He also used a Vision Board to focus on his desires. His Vision Board included images of everything that reminded him of New York City, including pictures of city landmarks, busy street scenes and brownstone buildings. His Vision Board was covered with affirmative statements such as, "I AM SUCCESSFUL AND PROSPEROUS IN EVERYTHING I DO!" and 'ALL MY PLANS, IDEAS AND INTENTIONS RESULT IN SUCCESS." He also gave up all feelings of anger and bitterness that he felt toward a former business partner knowing that negative feelings could block his manifestation. Although this was

challenging at first, he soon learned to overcome all negative feelings. As he did so, he felt better about manifesting the success he desired. In addition, twice a day Jacob repeated an Allowing Statement in front of a mirror. He said that it helped him quickly overcome the doubt and resistance that held him back in the past.

3) Lisa wanted a well-paying job after finishing college. Several times per day she repeated her Intention Statement, which was: "MY INTENTION IS TO HAVE A WONDERFUL JOB THAT MAKES ME HAPPY, UTILIZES MY TALENTS, AND PAYS ME WELL." In addition, she used Emotional Visualization each day. During these exercises, Lisa imagined working at her dream job, interacting with coworkers, and then she would imagine the satisfaction she would feel as she received her paycheck. Using a small card, she wrote down three of her favorite Emotional Visualization scenes, and she thoughtfully and feelingly imagined these scenes each day. She accelerated her manifestation by feeling grateful for her new job even before she got it. In order to maintain positivity and expectancy, she used the creative power of her spoken word each day. In fact, her favorite affirmation was, "I LOVE HAVING LOTS OF MONEY, AND IT NOW RUSHES INTO MY LIFE IN OVERFLOWING ABUNDANCE."

4) Stephanie's Intention Statement was, "MY INTENTION IS TO HAVE A LOVING, SUPPORTIVE, AND AWESOME RELATIONSHIP WITH A MAN WHO LOVES ME JUST AS I AM." Although she had a busy schedule, she always made time to repeat her statement throughout the day for the purpose of remaining focused and expectant. In fact, she wrote her Intention Statement on a small card and placed it near her computer so that she would be reminded to repeat it often. In addition, her favorite spoken affirmation to use throughout the day was, "I BELIEVE THAT I CAN EXPERIENCE LOVE AND ROMANCE RIGHT NOW. I SEE LOVE WHEREVER I GO, AND PERFECT LOVE NOW COMES TO ME IN PERFECT

WAYS AND IN PERFECT TIMING." Stephanie also used Emotional Visualization to help her feel the reality of her desires. She always started each session with a warm up exercise in which she would use her imagination and senses to remember something that made her feel good in the past. Once her feelings and senses were awakened, she would imagine what she would do, feel and say if she were in love with the perfect man. Stephanie also spent time looking at her Vision Board each day. The images and words on her board invigorated her and increased her expectation and faith in the manifestation process.

5) Michael used Emotional Visualization twice per day and repeated his Intention Statement several times throughout the day. After a month of commitment to his action plan, he felt that his Reticular Activating System was responding to his changing beliefs because he was becoming increasingly aware of events and circumstances that would help him manifest his desire for a loving relationship. During a telephone call one afternoon, Michael said to me, "After a month I felt like something in my mind had switched to automatic because I was suddenly feeling expectant about meeting the perfect woman for me. I was suddenly meeting lots of single women, and many of my friends even started introducing me to single women who were interested in romance."

Each of the five interviewees understood that daily, committed action is the most important element of manifestation. Although commitment to a Law of Attraction action plan is sometimes challenging, it becomes easier with each passing day. Many people give up a few days or weeks before their breakthrough occurs. This is why it is very important to remain committed and focused on using your action plan every day. One of the benefits of using the tools of manifestation is that they change the structure of your brain through the process of neuroplasticity. As you use Emotional Visualization and repeat affirmations for a month, for example, new neural pathways are created in your brain that make these exercises much easier with each passing day.

PART 5: Question and Answer Section

QUESTION: What should I do when I don't feel like repeating my Intention Statement?

ANSWER: You will not always feel enthusiastic about repeating your Intention Statement. Much of the time you will enjoy repeating it because it is designed to encourage hope and expectation, but occasionally you may not feel the desire to use your statement. For example, one day you might feel disinterested because you are tired or frustrated about something, but the key to accelerating your manifestation is to give attention to your intention as often as possible. As you do so, your committed action becomes a very strong affirmation to the Universal Law that you are persistent and committed to manifesting your desires. The Universe loves persistence and always rewards those who use the tools of manifestation on a daily basis.

QUESTION: Can I really manifest any desire with the Law of Attraction?

ANSWER: You can manifest anything that you can make a part of your beliefs and feelings, including friends, money, romance, a home, a luxury car, or the life of your dreams. In order to manifest your desires, it is very important to take a mental inventory of the things you want and then determine how you feel about them. Do you feel that you can have a new home, job or a successful life? Do you believe that you can manifest one million dollars by next year? If you don't feel comfortable having one million dollars, then how would a quarter of a million dollars feel to you? If you have trouble believing that you can manifest certain intentions, then you should use the tools of manifestation on a daily basis to expand your beliefs and feelings. As this happens, you will be in a better position to manifest exactly what you want. For example, a friend from Seattle, Washington, wanted to manifest one million dollars to provide his family with more financial stability. Two weeks after implementing his Law of Attraction action plan he called to say that he had trouble believing that he could have a million dollars. He said that his Emotional Visualization exercises were challenging because of doubt. I told him to start off by imagining how he would feel to have 50% more money than he was accustomed to, and then increase that sum over the following month as he felt better about having more money. After a few months he felt much better about his million dollar intention, and he even reported that his Emotional Visualization exercises were becoming easier and more enjoyable. As he persisted with the tools of manifestation, his life turned around rather dramatically, and he soon found himself running his brother's failing contracting business. With his creative ideas and marketing experience, he turned the failing business into a profitable enterprise. He now has much more money than the million dollars he originally wanted.

QUESTION: What is the difference between Affirmations and an Intention Statement?

ANSWER: Affirmations are statements of faith that are designed to generate positive and expectant feelings through constant repetition. A woman, for example, might enjoy repeating many different affirmations throughout the day. She might use various affirmations for love, success, confidence, forgiveness, and healing. A friend from Florida repeats a dozen different affirmations per day, some of which she has written herself. Her favorite affirmations are printed on index cards and placed throughout her house so that she will be reminded to repeat them throughout the day. An Intention Statement, on the other hand, is a single statement that serves the purpose of clarifying what we want to manifest. As we focus on our Intention Statement throughout the day, it helps us remain focused on our desires thereby calling into action the forces of creation. The Intention Statement keeps us focused and on track to manifesting our desires while affirmations help us maintain positive and expectant feelings throughout the day. A man might repeat many different affirmations throughout the day, but he will only have one Intention Statement.

QUESTION: How can I be sure that I am using the most effective Intention Statement for my desires?

ANSWER: Your feelings will confirm or deny that you are using the most effective Intention Statement. How do you feel about your Intention Statement? What emotions do you experience as you repeat it? Do the words feel believable to you? Does your Intention Statement call up feelings of expectation? If the words of your Intention Statement encourage you to feel positive and expectant, then you are on the right track. Don't fret about creating a perfect Intention Statement overnight; take your time, brainstorm, and find words and ideas that feel right for you. Feeling satisfied with your Intention Statement means that your desires are in alignment with your greatest expression of life. Also, do not limit your manifestation because you cannot imagine where you will get the money, the resources or the opportunities to manifest your desires. Your job is not to devise the ways in which your manifestation will come into your life, but it is to bring your thoughts, words, feelings and actions into alignment with your desires. We often limit our manifestations because we rely on logic or past experiences to define our future, out the Universal Law is not limited by these things. As a result, you should determine what you want, create it within your feelings, and then be open to receiving your desire from any avenue of expression.

QUESTION: How can I make my manifestation exercises easier to perform each day?

ANSWER: The best advice is to avoid going overboard by spending too much time using the tools of manifestation each day. A commitment of forty five minutes per day is all that you need to manifest your desires with the Law of Attraction. You should spend half your time using Emotional Visualization, and the remaining time should be spent using the other tools of manifestation covered in this book. If you commit to using the tools of manifestation for one or more hours per day, you are likely to become restless and then associate those negative feelings with the process of manifestation; however, frustration, negative feelings and procrastination is unlikely if you commit to smaller time increments. The old adage that "it's a cinch by the inch, but hard by the yard" is a good idea to keep in mind when using the tools of manifestation on a daily basis. In addition, you should take an inventory of your daily activities and determine where you can schedule your manifestation work with the least amount of effort. A female friend, for example, repeats her affirmations while running on her treadmill, and a man from Manchester, England, repeats his Intention Statement each morning while dressing for work. Another friend uses Emotional Visualization early in the morning before her family wakes up, and then in the evening she recites her Allowing Statement in front of her mirror before preparing dinner. She said that since committing to a Law of Attraction action plan, she has gotten two promotions at work, a free trip to Europe, and many more wonderful things. The purpose of these examples is to demonstrate that you can always find time to use the tools of manifestation, no matter how busy you are. The amount of time required to focus on and repeat an Intention Statement is about ten seconds. Each day you have 86,400 seconds at your disposal, so no matter how busy your schedule is you can always find time to use your Intention Statement and the other tools of manifestation throughout the day.

QUESTION: How will I know that I am adding enough emotion to my Emotional Visualization exercises?

ANSWER: During your exercises you should attempt to add as many tones of reality and emotion as you would experience if your desire was already your reality. If you want to have more money to save, spend and enjoy, then you should imagine how you would feel to have the sum of money you desire. If you had that dollar amount, how would you feel? Would you feel content, happy, and prosperous? Do not go overboard by adding too much emotion, but strive to feel exactly the way you would feel if you had the ability to buy all the things you want. How would you feel to visit a store and pay cash for one thousand dollars' worth of merchandise? Would you feel prosperous and financially free? If so, then center your attention on that feeling and imagine how you would feel to be prosperous and financially free. You can manifest the money you desire by capturing these feelings and maintaining them throughout the day. Keep in mind that feelings are very creative, so use them wisely because the Universe is always responding to the way you feel.

QUESTION: What if I don't feel like focusing on my Vision Board regularly?

ANSWER: Do it anyway. We all have commitments that we don't feel like doing occasionally, such as exercising or getting up for work on a Monday morning. The key to making the Law of Attraction work is to use it consistently no matter how you are feeling. As you start seeing positive results with your manifestation work, you will begin to feel positive and enthusiastic about using the tools of manifestation each day. This is the main reason I recommended a short, enjoyable warm-up session prior to your Emotional Visualization exercises. The positive feelings that you experience during these warm up sessions will rewire the neural pathways in your brain and thereby help you associate positive feelings with your manifestation exercises. The same information applies to using your Vision Board consistently. You should focus on your Vision Board even when you don't feel like doing so. A friend from San Diego, California, implemented a Law of Attraction action plan to manifest a lot of money to save and spend on the many things he enjoyed, such as going out to eat with friends, going to concerts, and taking vacations with his girlfriend. As he persisted in using the tools of manifestation each day, the things he desired started to show up in his life. Within a few months of committing to his Law of Attraction action plan, his life turned around in an amazing way. He said that the first few weeks were challenging because there were days when he did not feel like using the tools of manifestation, but his excitement and enthusiasm increased as he persisted in using the Law of Attraction each day. Eventually, his Law of Attraction action plan became an enjoyable part of his life. Although the Universal Law brought him money in ways that he could not have imagined, he also discovered a creative way to buy rare records and movie posters locally and then sell them online for profit. Through his dedication to the Law of Attraction, he began to earn an additional $3,000.00 per month consistently. These days he is living the life of his dreams because he persisted in using the tools of manifestation until his desires became his reality.

QUESTION: How long will it take to see results with the Law of Attraction?

ANSWER: If you are committed to using a Law of Attraction action plan you will begin seeing results in a relatively short amount of time. The results you experience will reflect your changing beliefs and expectation. At first you might see small results, but you should persist with your manifestation work until larger manifestations occur. It is important to acknowledge all manifestations no matter how small they are. Give thanks for the money you find, the discounts you get at stores, and the free meals offered by friends. Often, these are the first type of manifestations that appear when using a Law of Attraction action plan. In addition, you will invite more good things into your life by accepting everything that comes your way and by being thankful for all the good things that happen to you no matter how small your manifestations are at first. A friend from Vancouver, Canada, committed herself to an action plan that included the use of an Intention Statement, positive affirmations and Emotional Visualization exercises. She said that it was challenging to move past her old, limited ways of thinking at first, but as she persisted in using the tools of manifestation each day, things started to change for her. Doors started opening and opportunities appeared that enhanced the quality of her life. She made it a point to explain that she was thankful for each and every manifestation along the way no matter how small it was. Throughout the day she would take a few moments to give thanks for the money she was given, the free lunches she received, or anything positive that she experienced throughout the day. As she did so, larger manifestations appeared in her life, including a new career, a lucrative business, and many other opportunities. She is now living the life of her dreams because she added the necessary ingredient of action to the Law of Attraction.

QUESTION: Which manifestation tool is most important to use each day?

ANSWER: All the tools of manifestation are important, but you should focus on using the tools that make you feel positive and expectant. Men, for example, often excel with Emotional Visualization because men are emotionally wired in a way in which they are stimulated by images, pictures, and mental movies. Women, on the other hand, often excel with spoken affirmations because they are naturally in tune with the power of the spoken word and the feelings that words provoke. This does not mean that men cannot benefit from affirmations, nor does it mean that women cannot benefit from Emotional Visualization exercises. It means that each person should focus on the tools of manifestation that feel natural and most effective. For example, a woman who enjoys repeating spoken affirmations more than using Emotional Visualization might want to focus a majority of her energy on spoken affirmations and an Intention Statement. In addition, she might want to incorporate words and dialogue into her Emotional Visualization exercises to make this manifestation tool more enjoyable. A man, who is more stimulated by mental images than spoken words might want to focus a majority of his efforts on Emotional Visualization and the images on his Vision Board. The purpose of these exercises is to make you feel positive and expectant about manifesting your desires, so you should commit to using the tools of manifestation that make you feel positive and expectant each time they are used.

QUESTION: I feel that wanting lots of money and possessions is selfish and greedy. How can I overcome these negative beliefs?

ANSWER: It is very important to understand that your desire for more money is the result of an inherent evolutionary impulse to grow, learn and experience a more fulfilling life characterized by opportunities, choices, and pleasure. *There is very little fulfillment, spiritual growth and evolution in poverty and struggle.* The person with plenty of money, on the other hand, has a greater ability to enjoy the pleasures of life, such as travel, entertainment, shopping, and helping those who are less fortunate. As a result, you should start thinking about money as a way to buy the various experiences of life, such as books to edify your soul, a relaxing massage, tickets to a concert, or a well-deserved vacation. As you transform your feelings about money, you instantly liberate yourself from the false assumption that your desires are based in selfishness and greed.

PART 6: Creating & Implementing Your Daily Law of Attraction Action Plan

A Law of Attraction action plan is a powerful tool that can help you manifest anything that you can make a part of your beliefs and feelings. Unfortunately, some people fail to manifest their desires because they give up too soon or because they don't know what steps to take each day to make their dreams a reality. Therefore, the purpose of this section is to help you create and implement a Law of Attraction action plan that is effective and easy to use each day.

Many new students of the Law of Attraction become so excited about manifesting their desires that they commit to using the tools of manifestation for an hour or more per day. Unfortunately, this approach often results in boredom and burnout after a few weeks because it involves too much commitment within a short amount of time. The key to maintaining long-term commitment and enthusiasm is to follow a Law of Attraction action plan that is practical, enjoyable, and not very time-consuming. If you use the tools of manifestation correctly, and if all your thoughts, feelings and actions are in alignment with your desires, then 45 minutes per day is more than enough time to manifest your desires.

The best way to produce long-term success with your Law of Attraction action plan is to follow a schedule that allows you to incorporate the various manifestation exercises into your daily routine. A good example of this is a friend who admitted to using Emotional Visualization while sitting in her car during her fifteen-minute breaks at work. She could have taken a short nap or read the newspaper during her breaks, but she chose to use her free time in the pursuit of her desires. Another student of the Law of Attraction repeats spoken affirmations during her morning shower. Once she is dressed, she recites her Allowing Statement in the mirror before combing her hair and putting on makeup. In a similar manner, the author of this book repeats his Intention Statement and spoken affirmations while driving to and from work each day. Of course, you might be the type of person who is disciplined enough to set aside time to use all the tools of manifestation in one sitting, but this approach is often difficult for a majority of people who maintain busy schedules with work and family. Therefore, the most effective plan of action is to incorporate your manifestation exercises into your daily schedule so that they will become practical, convenient and enjoyable habits in the long run.

One of the most popular authors in the field of psychology is Dr. Maxwell Maltz, who wrote a very popular book titled Psycho-Cybernetics. In this 30 million copy best-seller, Dr. Maltz informed millions of readers around the world that it takes 21 days to establish a new habit. He based this information on observations with patients who demonstrated the ability to overcome negative conditioning and false beliefs within 21 days. Dr. Maltz was a strong believer in the idea that success and failure are habits, and those habits can be changed through positive thinking, self-affirmation, and visualization. As a result of his success in inspiring millions of people to create constructive habits, I have created a 21 day plan that will help you establish a habit of using the tools of manifestation on a consistent basis.

THE 21 DAY PLAN FOR DEVELOPING A LASTING HABIT:

PART 1, THE FIRST SEVEN DAYS: During the first seven days you should become familiar with using the various tools of manifestation, such as the Intention Statement, spoken affirmations, Emotional Visualization, the Belief Statement and the Allowing Statement. For example, after a short warm up session, you should spend five minutes with Emotional Visualization. Using your feelings and as many tones of reality as you can incorporate into this exercise, you should imagine what you would say, do and feel if your desires were a part of your life right now. Once you have spent five minutes with Emotional Visualization, you should spend an additional five minutes repeating spoken affirmations. Afterwards, spend a few minutes repeating your Intention Statement and your Belief Statement. Your final exercise for the first seven days is to recite your Allowing Statement in front of a mirror. As you perform these exercises, pay attention to how you feel. Does one particular exercise make you feel more positive and expectant than the others? On the other hand, do you feel resistance with one particular exercise, such as Emotional Visualization? If so, you might want to spend more time with this manifestation tool so that you will become more comfortable using it. In addition, as you familiarize yourself with the tools of manifestation for the first seven days, you should think about how you can fit these exercises into your daily schedule. If you are a morning person who seems to get a lot done before noon, then you might want to schedule a majority of your manifestation exercises for the morning hours. On the other hand, if you have a lot of free time during the evening you might want to schedule most of your manifestation exercises after dinner. The key to developing a lasting habit is to accomplish small things in great ways on a consistent basis.

PART 2, THE SECOND SEVEN DAYS: By this stage you should double your time spent using each manifestation exercise. For example, you should increase your Emotional Visualization exercise to ten minutes per day, which includes a few minutes of warm-up exercises as discussed previously in this book. In addition, by this stage you should be accustomed to using the tools of manifestation regularly and you should have a good idea about how you can incorporate these exercises into your daily schedule with the least amount of effort. In addition, by this stage you should have a good idea about how each exercise makes you feel. If you find that certain words, affirmations or imaginary scenes make you feel positive and expectant, then you should continue using them as part of your Law of Attraction action plan.

PART 3, THE FINAL SEVEN DAYS: At this point you should already have a good understanding of how to create a lasting habit, which includes a clearly defined action plan, the willingness to take small actions daily, and persistence. In addition, the time spent using these manifestation exercises should consume no more than forty five minutes per day. Also, you might want to create a written list of each manifestation exercise and basic information to help you remember the details of your daily action plan, such as the amount of time you will commit to each manifestation exercise, a list of your favorite spoken affirmations, and a short list of the imaginary scenes you enjoy using during your Emotional Visualization exercises. As you persist with these manifestation exercises, your Reticular Activating System will respond by making you more aware of the things that are important to you. For example, you will begin to notice people, situations and resources that will help you manifest the desires of your heart. As you begin to see positive changes in your life, your faith and expectation will increase. When this happens, your manifestation will appear in your life.

In closing, I want to stress that the Law of Attraction works if you work it, but you must work it daily, persistently, and whole heartedly. It will not respond to wishy-washy desires or half-hearted commitment, so you must be completely dedicated to making your dreams a reality. The Universal Law is a dynamic, expansive, and evolutionary force that is a part of every human being. Its aim is to provide you the spiritual insight and inspiration to evolve to a greater state of being, which is your spiritual destiny. You can have all the money, relationships, experiences and opportunities you desire, but you must understand that the price to pay is spiritual growth and evolution. The nature of this spiritual evolution is always forward, never backward, so once you say yes to this power you will step into a greater, more enlightened way of being. Once you say yes to spiritual evolution, you can never go back to your old ways of thinking and living because they will no longer work. At this point in life you will see clearly that the way out is always in, meaning that the way out of problems, challenges, and lack is to first go within your consciousness to create your desired reality. Once you understand your true spiritual destiny, you will be pleasantly surprised to discover that the Universal Law has been patiently waiting to say yes to you all along.

If you enjoyed this book, please check out my other books on Amazon.com:

Manifest Your Millions: A Lottery Winner Shares his Law of Attraction Secrets

How To Win The Lottery With The Law Of Attraction: Four Lottery Winners Share Their Manifestation Techniques

Made in the USA
Middletown, DE
25 August 2023

37357315R00033